# Survival:

## Learn To Survive Without Electricity During Power Outage

**Disclamer:** All photos used in this book, including the cover photo were made available under a Attribution–ShareAlike 2.0 Generic (CC BY–SA 2.0)

and sourced from Flickr

clarifying purposes only and are the owned by the owners themselves, not affiliated with this document.

## Table of Contents

## Introduction

You see on the news that there is a chance of flooding. Or perhaps you see that there is a tornado warning. If you live near the water you know that hurricanes or other tropical storms are a possibility. Basically, no matter where you live, you are at risk of some sort of natural disaster… followed by a power outage.

The problem is, you never know how long that's going to last. It could be an hour, it could be a day, or it could go on for days. You know that there have been times when a natural disaster could cause power outages for days at a time, and if the emergency is bad enough, you could find yourself on your own for this amount of time.

If you aren't prepared, this could turn into a disaster for you and for the people you love. If you don't know how to get the necessities you need in life, if you don't know how to cook or get the things you need, you could be in for a lot of trouble, and with no way to call for help.

That is when the panic sets in.

"How will I know my family is going to be ok?"

"How am I going to get food and water? Or what about shelter?"

"How am I going to make this last? Who knows how long it's going to take for this to clear out."

If you have wondered how you are going to manage these things, you are not alone. So many people are so used to the convenient lives they live, they don't know how to handle even the most basic functions in their day to day lives. Don't worry. This book is going to change all of that and give you what you need to survive any power outage that comes your way, no matter how long it lasts.

I am going to give you the skills you need to not only survive, but to live. You can face any power outage or natural disaster that comes your way with confidence, knowing that you are going to emerge on the other side perfectly fine.

Prepare and learn the skills you need, and you are going to be on top of your game when you are faced with any outage or blackout without stress or worry.

Let the troubles come, you got this!

## Chapter 1 – Power Outages 101

Most people have these ideas about how they are going to handle any form of disaster that happens. They assume no matter what goes wrong, they are going to be able to handle it, simply because they have watched their fair share of movies.

The fact of the matter is, you are going to be able to handle anything that comes your way, but you are going to have to make the right preparations for that to happen. Of course you can handle anything, but you are going to have to follow the directions to make the right preparations.

You are going to be fine, but follow the tips and tricks in this book to make sure you not only manage to get through your outage, but you will also be able to enjoy yourself while you do it.

**Everywhere on the planet is able to be hit with natural disaster, and when that happens, you run the risk of losing power. This can be long term or short term, but either way, you may be without power for a period of time**

No matter where you live, you run the risk of facing a power outage. You might be on the outskirts of some small town in the middle of nowhere, or you may be in the center of one of the biggest cities on the planet... no matter where you are, you could potentially lose power, and you may not know why, or for how long.

One of the biggest issues you are going to face when you run into a power outage is the panic that ensues. So many people do not know how to handle power outages, and when one happens, they are sent into a state of panic and don't know what to do.

One of the biggest things you can do is to remain calm, and be the beacon to your family. More often than not, a power outage is going to be due to something besides a natural disaster, but you are going to have to deal with many of the same issues either way.

**If the power goes out because of a natural disaster, the most important thing to do is make sure you are out of harm's way.**

Tornadoes are very straight forward — they happen then they are gone. Sure, you might have to deal with prolonged tornado warnings, but overall, they aren't that bad once the initial issue has passed.

What you have to deal with most often is the uncertainty of how long it's going to be out. Of course, you know you can live without the television or entertainment for any length of time you need to, but the real issue is going to be when it comes to the necessities such as food and water.

You are going to need ways to cook, access to fresh, clean water, and ways to maintain sanitation and good health.

If you are dealing with power outages due to things such as flooding, fires, or more dangerous natural disasters, make sure you are out of harm's way. If you are in danger of your house catching fire, or more flooding, you have to get somewhere safe.

Depending on the situation, you might have a safe place you can go to, or you might have to make due with what you find. Either way, safety needs to be your top priority before you move on to the basic survival skills you are going to need to have.

**Remember to always stick together with the others in your group. Situations can go from bad to worse if you split up, and you may not be able to find who you need to find.**

**When you stick together, you can take care of each other**

No matter how good of an idea it seems to be, you need to stick together. If it becomes absolutely necessary for you to move somewhere, move there together. The more you stick together, the better off you are going to be.

**Make sure you put together a survival kit, and that you keep your kit
up to date**

Survival kits may seem like paranoia, or like something you would think about putting together but never actually do, but trust me, once you have one in place, you are going to be set for life.

Survival kits can be purchased, but you are going to have a lot more control over what goes into yours if you make it from scratch, not to mention you will know without a doubt that you have what you need to withstand any power outage that happens.

Of course, you have to keep everything up to date and ready to go, so make sure you check the dates the items are going to be good until. This is going to apply to food and meds, and, of course, to the batteries you keep on hand.

In the next chapter, we are going to take a look at the things you should include in your survival kit.

All in all, with the right skills, power outages aren't hard to make it through. When you really think about it, so many people lived for years upon years without power, and you can, too.

You just have to know how.

## Chapter 2 – Your Supply List

When it comes to your survival and comfort during a long term power outage, the one thing that is going to help you more than anything else is the emergency kit you have on hand.

Sure, you may think that it's more manly to survive without anything on hand, but the fact of the matter is that it is a lot smarter to have the supplies you need right there when you need them, and you are going to be a lot better off if you do have them.

You can include the simple things in this kit that will make all the difference when it comes to how well you are able to make it through an outage, and there's no joking around with that.

**So, let's take a look at what you will need in your basic supply list**

First of all, the most important thing you can do when you are preparing for a power outage is to be optimistic about it.

While you may not want to deal with a power outage, and there isn't necessarily anything fun about dealing with a natural disaster or the power being out long term, it doesn't have to be the end of the world, nor does it have to be anything you are upset about.

If you know how to handle a variety of situations, and if you know how to maintain your basic quality of life regardless of whether or not you have power, a power outage really isn't anything to be worried about. All you have to know is how to manage your basics, and you are going to be just fine.

With the right tools.

Here are the things you need to include in any survival kit, and no matter how long the power is out, you are going to be just fine.

- **Canned foods** — Try to be diverse... you don't know how long the power is going to be out, so don't stock up on the same food, or you are going to risk having to eat the same thing for breakfast, lunch, and dinner for days on end.

- **Can opener... Make sure this is not electric!**

- **Bandages and basic medical supplies**

- **Water** – If you don't stock up on water bottles, make sure you get a water purifier

- **Flashlight and batteries**

- **Matches and fire starter**

- **Tracfone and battery powered radio-** just because you are out of power doesn't mean you have to be entirely off the grid... by keeping these things on hand you are going to maintain a connection to what is going on around the area

- **Keep non-electrical entertainment on hand** – You aren't going to spend the entire time surviving, so you are going to need some sort of entertainment on hand to keep occupied with during the down time

- **Hunting and fishing supplies** – Depending on where you are and the situation, you may find that you need to hunt or fish to get fresh meat sources for your food. Make sure you have these things handy and that you are able to use them effectively

- **Keep adequate clothing and blankets on hand** – hypothermia can set in faster than you can imagine. Keep enough on hand to warm up no matter what time of year it is

- **Keep sewing kits and repair kits on hand... whatever you have that may need repairs, make sure you have the supplies on hand to repair it**

Some of the things you find on this list may feel excessive, or they may seem like you wouldn't actually use them if you were in this kind of situation, but trust me, it's a lot better to have something on hand that you don't actually end up using than it is to need something and not have it.

You don't have to put your survival kit together in one day… I know these things can get expensive and you may not have the money to do it all at once. So don't worry about it!

If you add a little bit when you can, eventually you are going to have everything you need in stock for when the time comes. Plan your shopping trips around sales, and always buy things when they are cheap. If you buy some of the things you need at the end of camping seasons, you are going to save money.

If you plan your food storage around the bulk items at the store, you are going to fill your supply kit without any real impact on your budget. All you have to do is plan for the survival all through the year, and you will be ready if and when it ever happens.

You don't have to be paranoid about it, but if keep the possibility of such an occurrence on the back of your mind, you are going to be able to snap into action the moment it comes to life.

**When it comes to preparedness, you don't have to have a major impact on your day to day lives, all you have to do is plan a little here, and a little there.**

**The bits and pieces are going to add up over time, and before you know it you are going to have an entire survival kit set up and right where you need it to be**

Make sure everyone in your home knows where to find the kit, and no matter what happens, you are going to be ready for it.

There's no shame in being prepared, and with a kit on hand, that's exactly what you are going to be.

## Chapter 3 – The Skills Behind the Mask

Of course, everything you put in your survival kit is only as good as your ability to use it. You can keep your kit well stocked with all kinds of things, but unless you know how these things work, they aren't going to do you any good during a power outage.

So, for this chapter, we are going to take a look at the things you need to develop... basically, the skills you need to have are going to match what you put into your kit, but either way, these are skills you need for an outage no matter what.

Make an effort to develop each of these skills, and you are going to make it through any power outage you have to deal with. It may be a challenge to learn some of them, but trust me, the more comfortable you get with these skills, the easier it is going to be for you when the time comes.

- **Learn how to cook over an open fire** – One of the first things you will need is heat, whether this is to cook food, to purify water, or to keep warm. Of course, cooking over an open fire is the most important thing to do, but you need to know how to make a fire with wood and matches.

- **Make sure you know how to handle all of the manual maneuvers around your home** – we live in a modern age full of conveniences, but when the power is out, many of these conveniences no longer work. Make sure you know how to get around your house, and how to use the basic functions of your house without any power on at all

- **Plan your daily activities around the light you have available –** when you have no power, you don't have much of a light source available. Sure, you can use candles and flashlights, but when you don't know how long you are going to deal with an outage, it is smart to save these things for emergencies. Because of this, it's better to plan any reading or anything else you are going to do in the light during the day, then doing other activities when it gets dark

- **Learn how to hunt and fish for the things that are in your area –** you might be the mighty hunter when it comes to the big game in your area, but depending on the situation, if you are in a survival mode, you might have to settle for the little game that is in the area, which can be harder to harvest if you don't have the right kind of practice. Make sure you know how to hunt for the things that are available to you, and you will always have a food source on hand no matter what

- **Learn how to use the medical supplies you have on hand –** no one wants to think of stitches or broken bones, but when it comes to an emergency, you might have to deal with those very things. Make sure you know how to set a broken bone, how to administer the medication you have on hand, and how to use stitches if you need to. It is far better to know how and not need to rather than need to and not know how

- **Learn how to do the basic repairs around your house** – there isn't much you can do about the power, but if the roof breaks or if there's a broken window, you might have to bring out your skills to do some repairs around the place. You can do all kinds of simple repairs around the house that's going to save you a lot of work later on down the road.

- **Know how to use battery radios and try to have wind up generators on hand for times when you absolutely need light or to keep up on the news** – if you are in an emergency situation, you need to know what is going on in the outside world. There's no better way to do this than to have a radio on hand that you can operate by batteries or through a wind up generator. There are also flashlights you can wind up and use for when you need light.

You are going to find when you are in a survival situation, you have to combine your skills with the tools you have on hand. Of course, you can sharpen and prepare both of these things in advance, and I recommend you take the time to familiarize yourself with the things you keep in your kit.

You might not be great at first, and you might have to buy more of your supplies to keep some on hand in your kit, but the more you prepare, the better off you are going to be when the time comes for you to actually need it.

Confidence is key in many situations in life, and when it comes to survival, this is no exception.

Do what you need to do to build up your confidence, and you are going to be ready for anything.

## Chapter 4 – Tips and Tricks for Total Success

As with anything in life, there are definite things you should do, and other things you should not do during a power outage. Of course, some of these things need to be adjusted according to the situation you are in, and some of the things you are going to be able to decide as you experience it.

At the same time, there are definite things you need to do to know that will help you get through any outage that comes your way.

Here are a few of the things that are going to make your outage seem not so bad, and even somewhat enjoyable!

**First of all, get used to cooking... and I mean actually cooking... with foods you can open out of a can**

You can find entire dishes inside cans these days, including soups, chicken, and various kinds of meat, and veggies. When you are using your can opener and a pan, simply learn what combinations you enjoy, and you are going to be set.

If you want to get really fancy, you can always learn how to wrap your food in foil and nestle it in the coals of your fire... that's going to give you more of a baked effect for your dishes.

No matter how you are going to prepare your meals, make sure you diversify. Too many people get caught up in a rut and refuse to eat at all... a grave mistake when you are dealing with a life and death situation.

### Learn where you can find fresh water no matter where you are

There are various places around the house where you can find fresh water. You can find water in the back of the toilet, you can keep water in various places of your house, and you can keep water purifiers in your kit.

Make sure if you do store water that you rotate it throughout the year, this is going to ensure the water does not go stale before you get a chance to use it.

### Have safety places designated areas ready for when disaster strikes

Especially when you have a big family, you need to make sure you have a place for all of you to gather when you are in an emergency situation. Make sure everyone in your family knows where this spot is, and practice with everyone so everyone knows where it is when the time comes.

If you make any changes for any reason, make sure everyone is aware of this change. The last thing you want is to wonder where people are in the middle of an emergency.

### Have practice days to make sure you and everyone else knows what to expect

You can't always expect an emergency, but you can still give everyone in your family a heads up on how to handle it.

Make sure no one is going to panic and everyone knows how to handle themselves, or even give jobs to everyone so they know what they are supposed to do if you are in this situation. You can help everyone get prepared for what could happen so everyone knows what to expect when it does.

You don't have to be paranoid, and you don't have to always expect the worst, but with practice, you are going to be ready for anything.

## Chapter 5 – Common Mistakes People Make and How to Avoid Them

Up until now we have been focusing on how you can get ready for anything, and how you can have a survival kit ready for when you need it, but as with anything, there are some mistakes that you could easily make simply because you have never been in that situation before.

I want to help you avoid those mistakes as much as possible, and with this chapter, you are going to be able to do that very thing.

More often than not, you will be able to avoid making these common mistakes if you simply take the time to think about what you should do next. So many times, people rush into the decisions they make, especially when they are in critical situations.

Take a look at these common mistakes, and apply them to the situation you are in, and you will learn how to avoid them.

**One of the biggest mistakes people make in this kind of situation is that they don't properly assess the situation or their abilities**

Now, I'm not saying that you can't handle yourself, but what I am saying is that you are not a super hero, and you have to think things through before you do them. If the situation looks dangerous, it probably is. You have to be the one to be willing to walk away and let dangerous situations pass you by.

**Another common mistake people make is failing to understand they have to conserve the resources they have**

You know you are in a survival situation, and you know you know you have to be careful to survive, but you still have to make sure you have enough supplies to see you through for the long term.

You may be out of the situation in a few days, but you could be stuck in it for a few weeks. You never know how long it's going to take, so make sure you have enough resources to last.

**Don't make the mistake of thinking that you are just fine all alone. You have to do your part to keep up with the current events, and try to contact help, if possible**

This is why you need to use a battery powered radio if you can. You will be able to keep up on the current events, and be able to know where help is and what you should be doing. During power outages, the authorities and help are going to be doing what they can to get a hold of you and give you the directions you need.

**Don't make the mistake of going into areas you think you know when they have changed due to the outage**

For example, if you think you know your neighborhood, but the area is flooded, you may not actually know what is in the landscape. This means the area could pose more threats to you than what you think they would.

When you are in a survival situation, it is very important to stay on the side of caution, every time. When you are in an outage, you aren't going to have access to medical attention or other kinds of help, so you have to be really careful not to get hurt or put yourself in any more danger than what you are already in.

Of course, if you can take care of it, you are going to be better off than if you are completely unable to handle what comes up, but you still have to be careful. The safe you can keep yourself and your family, the better off it is going to be all around.

As I have said in the last chapter, this is nothing to be paranoid over, but you do want to be prepared. Blackouts happen, power outages happen, and things outside your control happen, but if you are prepared for the worst, things are going to turn out for the best.

## Conclusion

There you have it, everything you need to know to handle a blackout. I know it can be scary when the power suddenly goes out, especially when you have no idea how long it's going to be out, or how you are going to make your supplies last until it comes back on.

But, when you have the skills you need to make it through, you know you are going to be fine no matter how long it's out. Let this book give you the confidence you need to survive any power outage or natural disaster that comes your way, without worry that you aren't going to make it through.

When the time comes, you are going to have to be the strong one. People are going to panic, and they are going to wonder how they are going to make it through, and sometimes you just have to be the calm one in the eye of the storm. Let this book give you the confidence you need to be that calm one, and to push through whatever power outage you are faced with.

Whether you are dealing with an ordinary outage, or if you have to deal with flooding or tornadoes on top of it, you are going to be just fine. I know because you have the skills you need provided in this book. Let your fears and uncertainties fade as you sharpen your skills and prepare for the worst.

This book is designed to inspire, and with the skills you will find in this book, you are going to be inspired to make it through anything. So go ahead and run out to the store, gather the supplies you need, and practice the things you read in this book. The more you know, the better off you are going to be, and the less worried you are going to have to be when a storm hits.

Flooding happens, tornadoes happen, and all sorts of natural disaster happen, but the more you are prepared, the better off you are going to be. There's nothing wrong with being prepared, and the more you prepare for the power outages, the easier it is going to be for you to handle it when it does happen.

You have what it takes to survive, and you are going to make it out the other side a stronger person. Nothing is going to be able to hold you back.

Now get out there and power through the outage.

FREE Bonus Reminder

If you have not grabbed it yet, please go ahead and download your special bonus report *"Preppers Survival Guide. Proven Tactics For Armed Incounters!"*

Simply Click the Button Below

OR **Go to This Page**

http://preppersliving.com/free

## BONUS #2: More Free & Discounted Books & Products

**Do you want to receive more Free/Discounted Books or Products?**

We have a mailing list where we send out our new Books or Products when they go free or with a discount on Amazon. Click on the link below to sign up for Free & Discount Book & Product Promotions.

**=> Sign Up for Free & Discount Book & Product Promotions <=**

OR Go to this URL

**http://zbit.ly/1WBb1Ek**